THE CASINO AT MA

The Office of Public Works

INTRODUCTION

THE CASINO AT MARINO, LIKE SOME ANTIQUE SENTINEL, stands on a gentle rise just off the Malahide Road, outside Fairview, in north County Dublin. It is a building which ranks with the finest architectural compositions of Renaissance Europe. So often seen yet so seldom fully appreciated, the Casino is an architectural gem: small in scale, perfect in detail and proportion, and endlessly rich in subtleties. Within its simple and regular mass, four distinct and absolutely successful façades and over twenty interior spaces are to be found in a refined and intriguing composition.

The Casino, as a pure expression of architectural idealism, may be ranked with a small number of buildings of international significance. Its few peers include Andrea Palladio's Villa Rotunda at Vicenza (c.1567), and Inigo Jones's Queen's House at Greenwich (1619-22), both masterpieces of Renaissance architectural design. However, the Casino is not without an equal in Ireland. As a perfect miniature building, it has been compared to Cormac's Chapel, on the Rock of Cashel. Six centuries of cultural evolution separate these two buildings, but both remain as monuments to a country at its finest and to countrymen at their best.

A view by Thomas Roberts [formerly William Ashford] (1746-1824) of the Casino at Marino in its original setting. [Whitworth Art Gallery]

CHARLEMONT AND HIS ARCHITECT

THE CASINO WAS BUILT FROM ABOUT 1759 by James Caulfeild (1728-99), 4th Viscount Charlemont, later 1st Earl of Charlemont, widely recognised as one of the most enlightened and cultivated men of his day. As a man of the eighteenth century enlightenment, he loved his country and devoted himself to its social and cultural improvement, becoming the first Commander-in-Chief of the Irish Volunteers in 1780 and, in 1785, first president of the Royal Irish Academy. As a man of culture, he loved Italy, the centre of ancient Roman civilisation and the focus of its revival in the form of the Renaissance.

James Caulfeild, 1st Earl of Charlemont – portrait by William Cuming [NGI]

Convinced of the need to live in his own country, yet wanting to retain the inspiration of Italy, Charlemont attempted to bring a part of it to Ireland. He acquired the Marino estate in 1756 and set about the re-formation of the demesne in an Italian style.

Over the succeeding years it was landscaped by the Irishman Matthew Peters who had trained at the gardens of Stowe in Buckinghamshire. The new estate was dominated by the relaxed and informal English landscape tradition which reached its height with Capability Brown. This was a style of environmental modelling inspired by the seventeenth-century idealised Italian landscape views by Nicolas Poussin and Claude Lorraine. Soft undulating and open, with clumps of trees carefully dispersed to give scale to the estate's extent, the lands created the relaxed setting for many of the ornamental buildings of the Marino demesne and particularly for the classical formal discipline of the Casino.

The Casino was the *chef d'oeuvre* of the estate and, costing some £20,000, by far the most expensive of its various ornaments. As a garden building in the antique style it displayed the architectural idealism expected of its small scale and decorative role. The Casino was also a temple to Charlemont's social and cultural ideals. These were re-interpreted, after the fashion of the day, in the symbolic language of antique gods. With statues of Ceres and Bacchus on the north or entrance front, representing the harvest and good living, and on the south front Apollo and Venus, gods of the muses and of love, Charlemont's Casino was dedicated to the finest ideals of eighteenth century society. Culture and agriculture were united, and these themes were to recur in the interior decoration.

It was only inside the Casino that the building's final role was revealed, for the Casino was also a residential summer house and belvedere. From here one could view the landscape in the most sumptuous surroundings, and provide formal and informal entertainment as required. Reception rooms, private rooms, bedrooms and attendant facilities are all arranged within its three-storey interior. We might even add to this a fourth storey, as the roof was left flat so it could form a viewing platform, providing an even more expansive view of the district. Regardless of familiarity, it is always a surprise to find this variety of interiors in a building which, externally, betrays only one floor and suggests only one room.

To say that the Casino perfectly satisfies all of its roles – ornamental, symbolic and residential – is the greatest tribute one can pay its designer. In about 1757, Lord Charlemont engaged as architect William Chambers (1723-96), whom he had befriended in Rome in the early 1750s. Chambers was later to become the most highly regarded architect of his day. The brilliant imagination of this young architect, still only in his mid-thirties when he designed the Casino, was given full scope in the manifold problems of the commission. Not only did he provide a design fulfilling all the requirements of its patron, but one which successfully embodied the most avant-garde principles of architectural design. Indeed Chambers himself realised the significance of the Casino and published it as the first plate of his designs in his *Treatise on Civil Architecture* of 1759. Here it represented not only Chambers's abilities as an architect, but exemplified his ideals of disciplined architectural design.

Sir William Chambers
– portrait by Sir Joshua Reynolds [RA]

CHARLEMONT'S TWO LOVES: IRELAND AND ITALY

As Lord Charlemont's idea in the development of his suburban estate was to recreate an Italian arcadia in Ireland we might well consider what motives he had for this ambitious project. The two over-riding loves of his life were Italy, particularly ancient Roman Italy, and Ireland. Later he wrote – 'I may love Italy as a mistress, while my native country claims from me the proper and just regard due to a wedded wife.' The reasons why he held these two countries in such high esteem were intimately linked with his background and with contemporary Irish and European society.

Charlemont's love of Ireland was founded on his family's historic association with the country. His family, the Caulfeilds, had been in Ireland since the beginning of the seventeenth century when Toby Caulfeild, later 1st Baron Charlemont, was placed in charge of Charlemont Fort in County Armagh. Throughout the seventeenth and early eighteenth centuries, the family advanced itself in Irish society. James, the 4th Viscount and builder of the Casino, fully appreciated his historic links with his natural homeland: 'I, being thoroughly sensible that it was my indispensable duty to live in Ireland, determined by some means or other to attach myself to my native country ...'

Charlemont's self-imposed duty to Ireland was one of the most distinguished facets of his character. Throughout his life, his devotion to the improvement of Irish society and culture determined his principles and his actions. Politically his ideas were liberal and nationalist, at least in their eighteenth-century context. They were, perhaps, best summarised in his attitude to his Marino estate. The demesne was left unwalled and open to the public, a feature unique in Ireland for its time. His estate was not only a private garden but a contribution to the civic grandeur of the capital and the country. The gesture, rooted in Italian precedent, was greatly appreciated by the city. One contemporary reported in 1783 'The utmost liberality of admission is permitted here; the inhabitants of Dublin may at all times amuse themselves with an agreeable walk.'

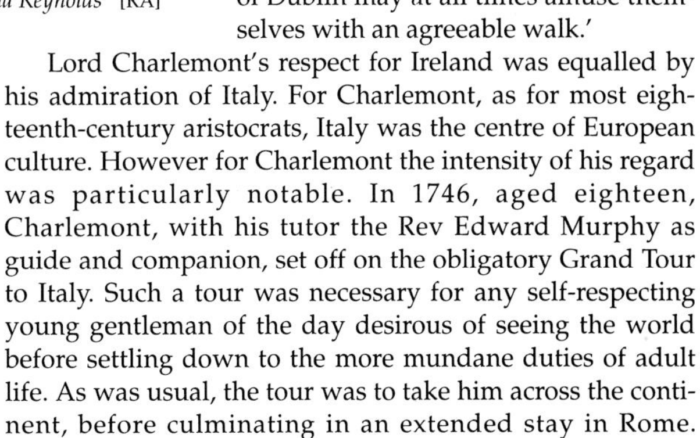

Lord Charlemont's respect for Ireland was equalled by his admiration of Italy. For Charlemont, as for most eighteenth-century aristocrats, Italy was the centre of European culture. However for Charlemont the intensity of his regard was particularly notable. In 1746, aged eighteen, Charlemont, with his tutor the Rev Edward Murphy as guide and companion, set off on the obligatory Grand Tour to Italy. Such a tour was necessary for any self-respecting young gentleman of the day desirous of seeing the world before settling down to the more mundane duties of adult life. As was usual, the tour was to take him across the continent, before culminating in an extended stay in Rome.

What was unusual about Charlemont's tour was the inclusion of the Greek islands on his itinerary. At Corinth, he saw 'a most noble and poetick view of Parnassus and Helian in the snow', and he made measured drawings of the plan of the Parthenon at Athens. The inclusion of these exotic and dangerous locations in his itinerary exemplified his advanced and wide-ranging interest in culture and antiquity.

After touring Europe and the Mediterranean, Charlemont stayed in Italy for some four years from his final arrival there in 1750, mixing in society, meeting artists and collecting art-works and books. During this time he encountered and befriended four artists who were to figure in his later creations: William Chambers, the architect, Simon Vierpyl and Joseph Wilton, sculptors, and Giovanni Battista Cipriani, an artist and decorator. Charlemont's magnificent art collection (now dispersed) also dated largely from this period when he expended vast sums on antique and modern works. These were shipped back to Ireland and stored, often still in their crates, in his family home in Jervis Street or simply left in the Custom House to await his return.

Charlemont and his circle caricatured by Joshua Reynolds in a parody of Raphael's 'School of Athens' (1791) [NGI]

In 1754 Charlemont began preparations for his return to Ireland. In that year Thomas Adderley, second husband to Charlemont's mother, offered him a house and estate at Donnycarney, which Charlemont accepted and renamed Marino. Stretching to the shores of Dublin Bay, it was both convenient to the city, in accordance with Charlemont's public duties, and salubrious, satisfying the requirements of his irregular health. Thus it was a suburban estate proper, after the Italian fashion, a country residence near the city. The estate further recommended itself to Charlemont as its new-built house (now demolished) contained a long gallery which, as Adderley pointed out to Charlemont, was 'suitable to house your growing collection of antiquities'.

The year 1755 marked the genesis of the Casino with the earliest documented discussions of Charlemont's intentions to build a temple on his own estate. In April of that year Charlemont corresponded with the Dutch-Italian architect Luigi Vanvitelli (1700-73) regarding the design of a temple. Vanvitelli's demands for the design were considered 'extravagant'. Instead Charlemont, some time between 1756 and 1757, turned to his old Roman acquaintance, William Chambers, to provide the design. The young Irish peer's intuition proved correct for Chambers provided a design which embodied the highest principles of antique classical design.

WILLIAM CHAMBERS: DESIGNER OF THE TIMES

However idealistic and extravagant Charlemont was in the creation of the Casino at Marino, all would have been wasted had he not selected a genius of the stature of William Chambers as his architect. The son of a successful Scottish merchant working in Sweden, Chambers was born there in 1723. At the age of sixteen he joined the Swedish East India Company but after a decade of travel he turned to architecture as a career.

Late in 1749 he went to Paris to study after which he moved to Rome to gain an understanding of its ancient grandeur at first hand. There he met Lord Charlemont who was to become his most important private patron, surpassed only by the English royal family. Chambers finally left Rome in 1755, returning to England to establish his practice in London. In 1757 he gained royal recognition with his appointment as an architect to the Dowager Princess Augusta and as tutor to her son, the Prince of

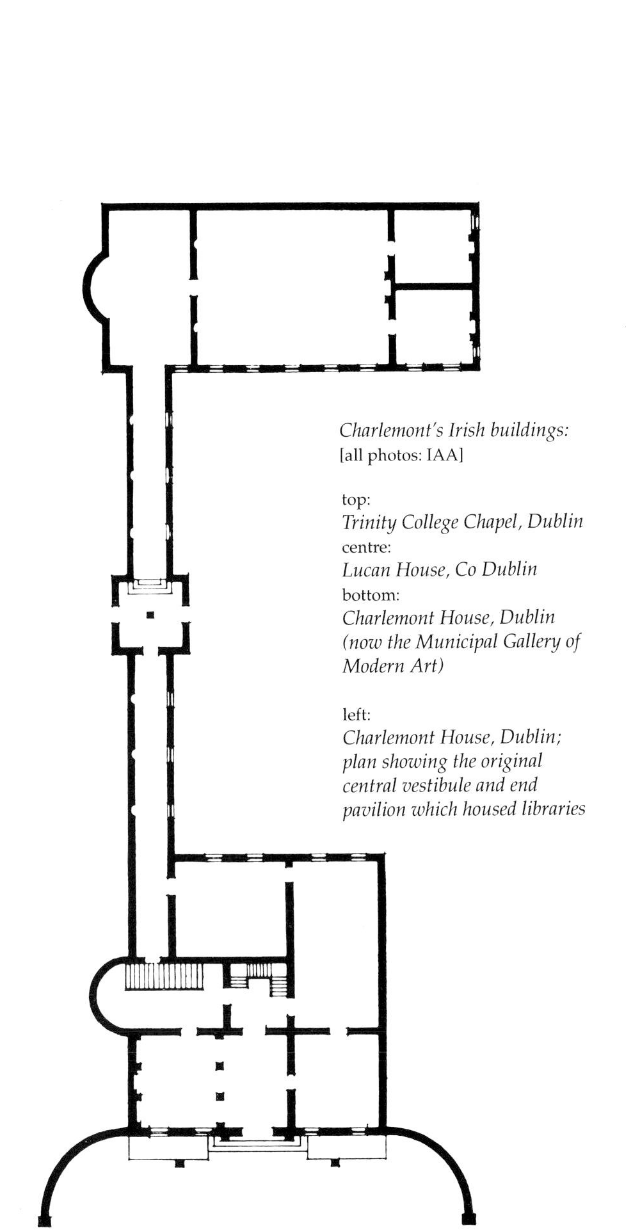

Charlemont's Irish buildings:
[all photos: IAA]

top:
Trinity College Chapel, Dublin
centre:
Lucan House, Co Dublin
bottom:
Charlemont House, Dublin (now the Municipal Gallery of Modern Art)

left:
Charlemont House, Dublin; plan showing the original central vestibule and end pavilion which housed libraries

Wales. The Princess employed Chambers to enliven her gardens at Kew with architectural ornaments. His experiments there in small-scale architectural design, both exotic and classical, provided him with an essential background to face the formal problems of the commission for the Casino at Marino.

After 1759, and the publication of the first edition of Chambers's magnum opus *The Treatise on Civil Architecture*, he quickly established himself at the head of his profession. Lucrative royal and private commissions followed, including the re-modelling of Buckingham House, now the palace, and, less exclusive but more representative, Charlemont House in the centre of Dublin (1763), now transformed into the Municipal Gallery of Modern Art in Parnell Square. In 1775, Chambers's career took a dramatic turn as he was appointed architect to the most extensive public commission of the day, Somerset House. As a professional architect, it was to be the crowning achievement of his career but it could never compare with the summit of his art, Charlemont's Casino.

The Casino was the supreme expression of Chambers's early influences from Paris and Rome. Its design, as Chambers noted in a later edition of the *Treatise* (1791), was derived from an unexecuted design for 'one of the end pavilions of a considerable composition, made soon after my return from Italy ... for Harwood House'. In both the Casino and its model, the free-standing columns, square proportions and heavy attic elements define the main elevations. Chambers's French, structural concerns dominate and what Robert Adam called his 'more architectural than picturesque' taste reigns supreme. From his Roman experience comes the antique inspiration in the decorative details. The lions *couchant*, originally intended as fountains, the rich detailing of the architectural elements and the funerary urns as chimneys all indicate a robust Roman inspiration unsullied by the lighter, more decorative traditions of the Renaissance. Roman grandeur continues inside where heavy coffered and compartmented ceilings rise from strongly detailed entablatures in the vestibule and saloon. Antique authority in detail was combined with contemporary structural concerns to create the Casino. Such a triumph could only have occurred with a uniquely sympathetic patron. That sympathy was evident in lines penned by the ill and aged Charlemont on hearing of his old friend's death in 1796 –

TO
Sir William Chambers, Knight, Etc.,
Fellow of the Royal Academy,
And Professor of Architecture,
The Best of Men, and the First of English Architects,
Whose Buildings, Modelled From His Own Mind,
Elegant, Pure, and Solid,
Will Long Remain the Lasting Monuments
Of That Taste,
Whose Chastity Could Only Be Equalled
By The Immaculate Purity of The Author's Heart,
James Earl of Charlemont, His Friend,
From Long Experience of His Worth and Talents,
Dedicates This Inscription
To Him And Friendship

The Wheatley engraving of the Casino at Marino, dated 1782

BUILDING THE CASINO

THOUGH ALWAYS PROUD of his designs for the Casino, Chambers's later employment did not allow him time to travel to Ireland to see his executed design. It is certain that Chambers's supervision of its construction was impossible. This task then fell to another of Charlemont's artist-friends from his Roman sojurn, an English sculptor, Simon Vierpyl (c.1725-1810).

Vierpyl was to be involved in some of the most important public and private buildings in the capital. Both the Royal Exchange (1769), now the City Hall, and the Blue Coat School (1773), now the headquarters of the Incorporated Law Society of Ireland, were built with his participation.

Vierpyl's European experience of stonework and building techniques allowed him to pass on this knowledge to his Irish workers and to make an important contribution to the tradition of building in Ireland. He was responsible for the supervision of the Casino's construction and the superb detailing of the Portland stonework, so much a part of the real character of the Casino.

Chambers's penchant for extravagant Roman decorative detail only added to Vierpyl's challenge. Chambers himself acknowledged Vierpyl's skill when he wrote of the Casino that it 'was built by Mr Verpyle [sic] with great neatness and taste'.

The state room has also been linked with Vierpyl. This room, almost hidden away on the first floor, has no documented connection with Chambers and, though his designs indicate the intention of having a first floor in the Casino, the details lack the sophistication of Chambers's hand. The elaborate interior of the state room may have been conceived by Chambers but detailed by Vierpyl.

LATER HISTORY

In 1783, Thomas Milton published a view of the Casino in its grounds with an accompanying text stating that 'The Foundation of the Casine, was laid by the present Noble Proprietor some time either in the Year 1761 or 62. A Brass Plate was fixed in the first Stone, with the Date engraved...' He went on to say that 'The Inside is not yet quite finished, but wants very little of being completed.' By Milton's account at least twenty-one years passed in the building and completion of the Casino. Later research into the Casino's history suggests that this impressive span should be increased, for in 1759 Chambers described the building as 'now erecting' and a report in *The Irish Times* of 16

The Irish Croquet Championships at the Casino, Marino, 1874 [Croquet Association of Ireland]

September 1886 refers to a receipt for a model of the Casino dated February 1758. If we include the gestation period, we can extend its life back to 1755 when Charlemont requested the designs for a temple from Luigi Vanvitelli. In effect, for just under half his long life, Charlemont was involved with the planning and development of his temple.

One of the reasons for the slowness of the building process was the financial difficulties faced by Charlemont during the 1770s, difficulties which were to recur throughout his later life. These also contributed to Chambers's later retreat from Charlemont's continuing building activities. As late as 1779 Chambers was reminding Charlemont of bills unpaid, dated 1773 and 1775, totalling £60. Included was a bill from May 1773 for 'Drawings and Directions for painting the Vestibule of the Casino' for which Charlemont was being charged £2 2s.

While it might be fairly asked if Charlemont ever really finished the Casino it was at least habitable by the mid-1770s. By this time he had completed his major outlays on its furnishings. This allowed Charlemont some quarter of a century enjoyment from his creation.

With Charlemont's death in 1799, his extravagant building and collecting had left his estate in dire financial circumstances. His son and successor Francis, 2nd Earl of Charlemont, was directed to sell everything to clear the debts. All, that is, but the house in the city, with its extensive library, the Casino with thirty acres and Marino House, where the Earl's widow the dowager Lady Charlemont was to live until her death in 1807.

In 1802, the 2nd Earl let the Casino to a local man, William Jolly, who held it until the 1830s. After its reversion, the estate, which had fallen into disrepair, was put back in order.

However, in 1864-65, with the death of the 2nd Earl and the succession of his nephew to the title, the Charlemont estate in Dublin went into its final decline. The 1st Earl's library, described by Maurice Craig as 'the finest private library that Ireland is ever likely to see and one of the finest ever brought together on this side of the Atlantic', was sent to auction almost immediately. In 1870 the town house was sold to the Government, becoming first the General Register and Census Offices for Ireland and later, the Municipal Gallery of Modern Art.

In 1881 the Marino estate was sold and the Casino fell into disrepair. Its rescue began in 1930 when an act was specially framed to allow the Casino to be taken into state care. Essential repairs were made to the fabric and the building secured in anticipation of its future restoration. Some work was undertaken in the 1950s and 1960s though the Casino's present re-instatement was not begun until 1974. This work spanned almost a decade until the re-opening of the Casino in 1984.

The Casino

From a distance the apparent simplicity of the Casino is its most striking feature. Its character is essentially sculptural, like some antique monolith carved into a classical cubic block. In fact, in many ways it is a piece of sculpture, with its small scale – only some fifty feet square to the outer columns – and its monumental proportions, enhanced by the apparently solid attic block.

The base from which the Casino rises, guarded by lions, is like a pedestal to a sculpture, gently but firmly raising the building above the surrounding land. Set on this comparatively severe plinth is the Casino itself.

In plan it is a Greek cross, with four equal arms. Each projecting face of the cross is framed by pairs of columns. These columns are emphatically freestanding to clearly stress their structural role. At the corners four more columns define the square body of the Casino. No superficial decoration disturbs the distant view. Only the two urns set on the attic might suggest a gratuitous disturbance of the sculpted block. But they give the silhouette its classical character and, as disguised chimneys, they have an undeniably practical function.

On approaching the Casino its sturdy proportions are preserved but the emphatic modelling of the building becomes increasingly evident. Plain columns contrast with broad planes of channelled stone walls, while the surrounds to the openings become increasingly significant. The carved details in the frieze with its ox-skulls and shields, the balustrade above, the garlands on the faces of the attic panels, all these and more continue to engage the interest of the spectator. The building, though still solid and sturdy, has opened out more to reveal a character rather different from a square block.

The four sculpted gods, Bacchus, Ceres, Apollo and Venus, break the silhouette against the sky, while the corner columns create architectural spaces which can be experienced without actually entering the building. This is particularly evident in the south front where two flights of steps give access only to the external corner spaces of the building. Throughout the Casino one should always be prepared to look up – it is there, on the undersides of surfaces, that some of the richest ornament is often to be found. The decorative carving, exquisitely detailed, provides the visual interest in close observation. Executed to the highest standards, the finesse of the carving set new standards in Ireland.

The sculptural ornament – the attic urns and the urn to the south, the four lions, (probably by the English sculptor Joseph Wilton), and Cipriani's panels with fauns below the lions – are works of art in their own right. Perfectly composed and, as one would expect from Chambers, Charlemont and their circle, inspired by Roman types, they draw the visitor around the Casino.

THE ELEVATIONS

Indeed circling the Casino one becomes aware of how its apparent simplicity belies a remarkably complex exterior, for the Casino's four fronts are, on close inspection, each unique. The entrance front and south front are distinguished by the attic storey with statues and urns, though the north elevation, with its grandiose doorcase rising to almost the height of the columns, is more dramatic. The east and west fronts are treated as minor elevations, with small triangular pediments. But these are different, as the west front has windows flanking the central wing. This restrained variety, with Chambers delighting in his own ingenuity, continues inside.

The main entrance to the Casino was intended to provide the first and most dramatic of the building's many surprises. While the monumental pedimented entrance doorcase echoes the scale of the exterior, the Casino could be entered by a two-leafed door which only rises half-way up the outside door. This change of scale between exterior and interior was charged with drama and revealed the ultimate artifice of the whole design.

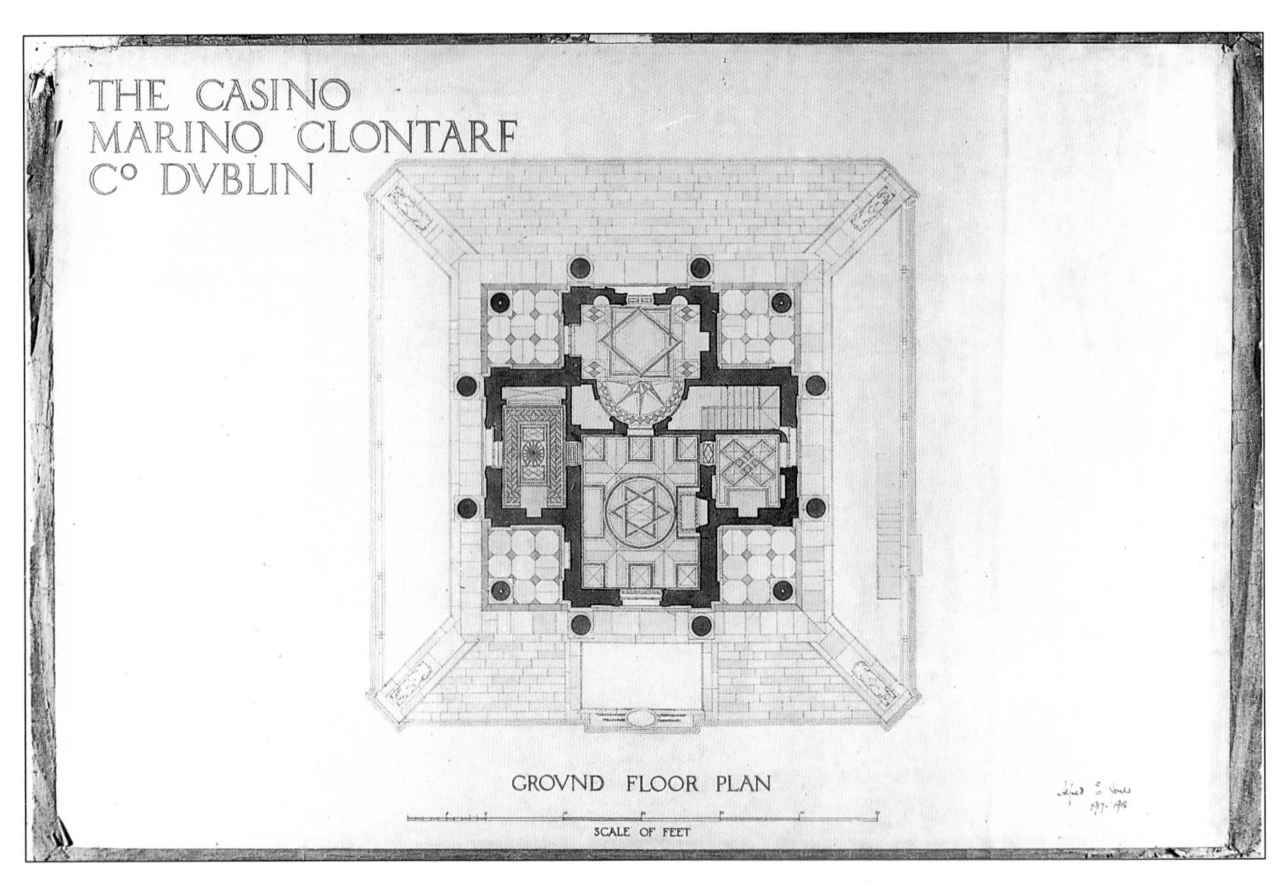

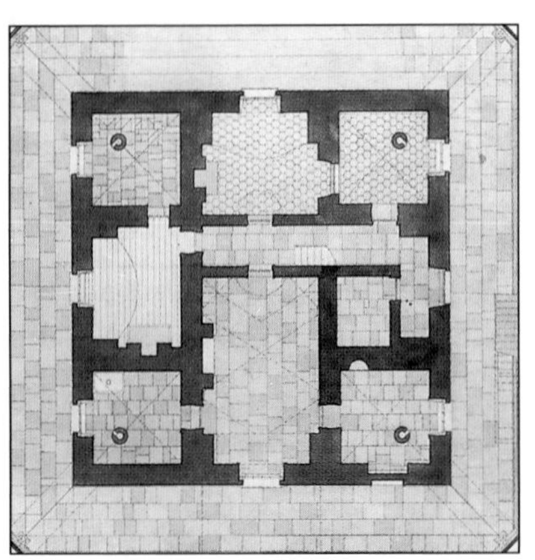

The Casino at Marino

above: *Ground Floor Plan*
left: *Basement Plan*
right: *First Floor Plan*
[Alfred E. Jones, 1917-18]

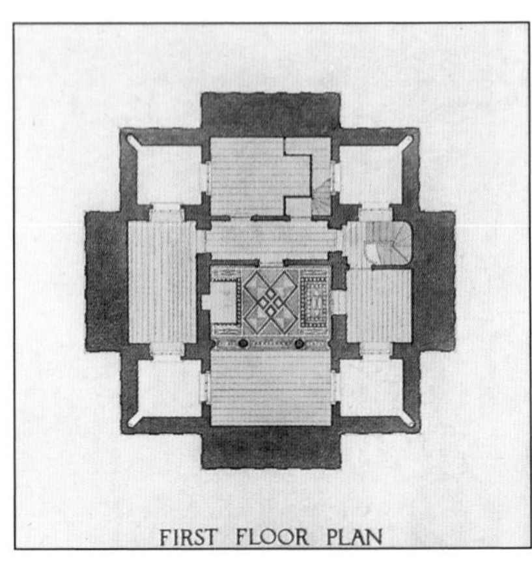

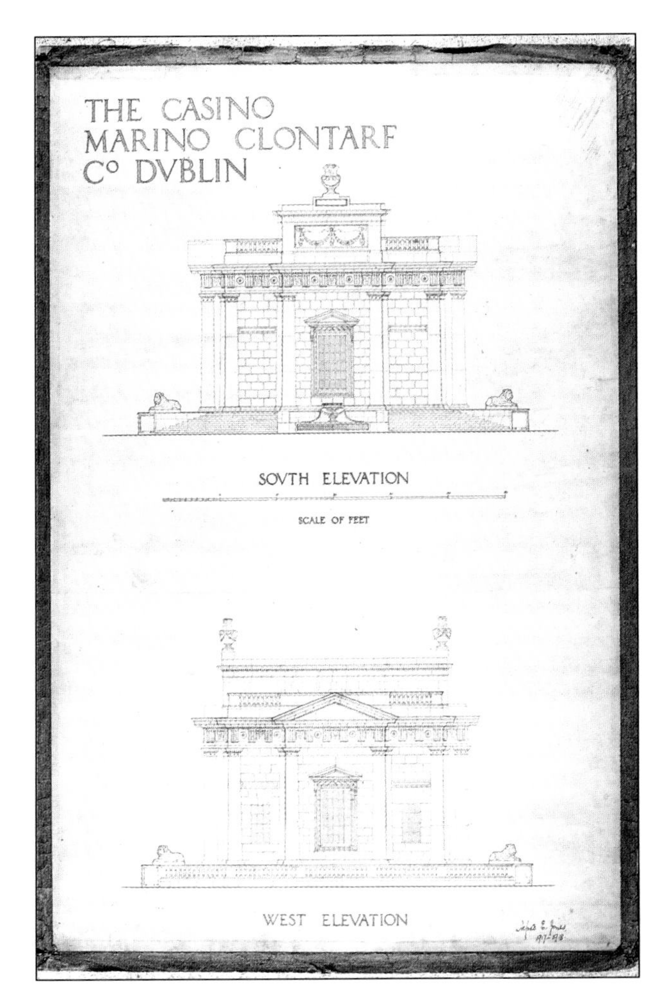

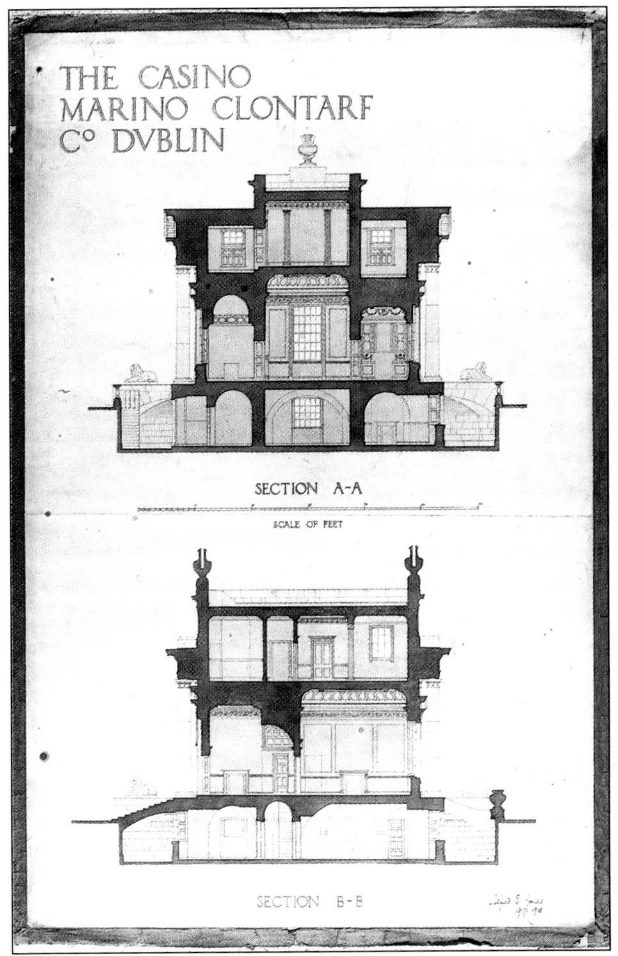

The Casino at Marino

left: *South and West Elevations*
right: *Sections*

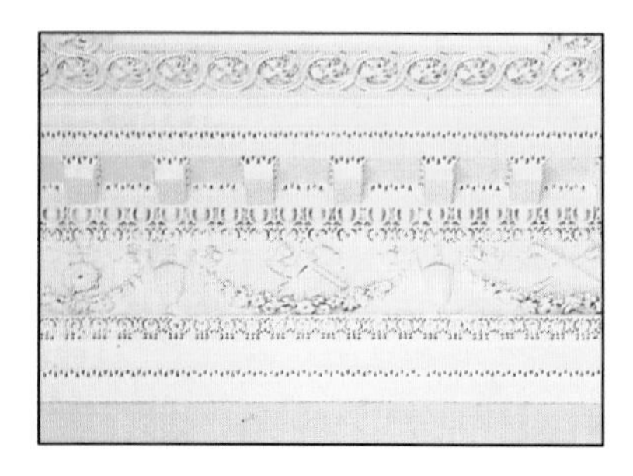

THE HALL

The hall or vestibule sets the mood for the rest of the interior arrangement and, with its spatial variety, classical references and small scale, it seems to be part of a quite different building. For all its smallness, it is filled with architectural elements. Composed around its walls are four doors, a window, a fire-place and two niches. However, here, as throughout the structure, the proportions are sensitively assessed so that any impression of crowding is avoided.

This room is relatively formal, befitting its role as the introduction to the interior. It is imbued with a formal architectural discipline eased by the scale and the wealth of ornamental detail. The rich carving of the door-frames has few equals in the country. The carved dado or chair-rail is set with a wave-like pattern, the Vitruvian scroll, enriched with flowers. The interior's cool white colour, with oils on the joinery and distemper on the plaster, reinforces its discipline and gives variety to its different surfaces. In contrast the magnificent parquet floor, using exotic woods patterned in geometric and possibly symbolic shapes, evokes a different mood. While here, as throughout the Casino, the floors might be considered too distracting, the original furnishings would have eased their effect. In the hall, now-lost monochrome paintings by Cipriani and Charlemont's sculpture display would have helped balance the attraction and interest of the floors.

The plaster ceilings and decorative details are particularly distinguished, with a coffered or panelled ceiling rising over the semi-circular apse and a compartmented ceiling over the rectangle. The square coffers of the apse diminish in size as they rise, with a corresponding reduction in their mouldings, enhancing the perspective and increasing the sense of space. The five-compartmented ceiling carries a central plaster trophy of classical motifs, including the lyre of Apollo, god of the muses. The theme is carried into the frieze where urns linked by garlands frame pairs of musical instruments.

opposite: *The semi-circular apse of the hall with curved doors either side of the entrance to the saloon*

THE SALOON

The main apartment of the Casino is the saloon, decorated in blue and white with the silk hangings secured by a striking gilded border. Above the walls, on a white curved or coved ceiling set with hexagonal coffers, a single compartment in light blue contains Apollo's head appearing from a sun-burst. The colour scheme of this room is based on the detailed scientific analysis of the remains of the original scheme. This restoration is one of the most complex aspects of the Casino's re-instatement. Using some one hundred paint samples, limited historical documentation and comparable surviving interiors, the decorative scheme of the room has been re-created as far as possible.

The original colour scheme was finalised in 1769 after Chambers wrote to Charlemont, in a letter of 22 March of that year, recommending 'that the Entablature, door(case) etc of the room should be dead white touched with blue and that the cove parts of the ceiling ... be of a more brilliant white'. Careful examination of the surviving material showed that the painting of the carved enrichments followed this scheme, with a fairly high-gloss blue picking out the flat finish of the white. The blue highlighting, both in the original and in the restoration, was applied quite loosely, purposefully avoiding the strict correlation of painted and carved details.

The loss of the original furnishings has been particularly significant in the saloon, as its colour scheme was related to ornaments, using the semi-precious blue stone lapis-lazuli on the two most important furnishings of the room. The original chimney-piece was an elaborate white marble creation by Francis Harwood. It featured a plaque, 12" x 5", of lapis-lazuli and was carved by Harwood in Italy about 1768. The chimney-piece was balanced on the opposite side of the room by an equally elaborate table with a lapis-lazuli top made by Joseph Wilton in London in 1773. Both disappeared without trace in the nineteenth century, without any further clues as to their design, leaving the room without its most elaborate furniture.

opposite: *View of the saloon showing the elaborate parquet floor and coffered ceiling. The outline of the gib door can also be seen.*

The arrangement of the saloon was significantly modified by Chambers and Charlemont during construction. Chambers originally intended five doors ranging along the walls: the door from the hall, two giving access to the flanking rooms in the side-arms of the Greek cross plan and two more false doors, responding to this pair, adjacent to the south wall. Had this been carried out it would have resulted in a room as heavily articulated as the hall. Instead, in 1768 and at Charlemont's own suggestion, it was decided to eliminate the false doors and to use hidden doors or gib-doors to the lateral rooms. Thus the interior was dramatically altered to become one of monumental simplicity with, apparently, only one door.

THE CHINA CLOSET AND ZODIAC ROOM

The china closet occupies the western arm of the Casino's plan highlighting the small scale of the building. Originally intended as a bedroom, its modern title originates in the early nineteenth century, when the second Lady Charlemont appropriated it to her own use. Certain details of the decoration, particularly the interlaced vines of the frame to the arched recess, clearly indicate some Victorian alterations. However, the precise reason for these alterations and their extent is uncertain.

The ceiling and cornice are particularly notable survivals from the original scheme. The cove of the ceiling is ornamented in accordance with Charlemont's agricultural ideals. Here, hanging garlands frame rustic variants of antique trophies. Instead of the ancient Roman shield, spear and sword we find devices like the rake, spade and scythe. Once again the symbolic language of antiquity is exploited to proclaim Charlemont's distinguished and enlightened ideals.

The arched recess to the north contains floral paper from Rathbeale Hall, Co Dublin. This Chinese-style wallpaper of c.1750, determined the reserved colour scheme of the walls as the colour of the paper's ground is extended over what are thought to be the later decorative alterations

left: *The china closet*

to tone down their rather inappropriate presence. The recess itself was not indicated in Chamber's published plans of 1759 and its introduction is associated with one of the most interesting and complex aspects of the Casino's design. However, the reason for its presence can only be found in the arrangement of the opposite, eastern arm.

As the zodiac room or study shares the eastern arm of the plan with the staircase, its space is much more constricted, though the confinement of the interior is eased by the presence of the dome. Below the dome, the signs of the zodiac can be found, giving the room its more atmospheric title. The small scale of this room results in it being lit by only part of the external window. This allows one side of the window, the northern panes extending behind the wall opposite the fireplace, to light the adjacent staircase. This ingenious if somewhat artificial device ensures the proper lighting of the staircase without any disturbance of the external elevation. In a singularly severe logical development it also provides an explanation for the presence of the arched recess in the china closet.

In the published designs, the wall separating study and staircase was slightly to the north of its present position and the study received all the light from the window. However, in execution, the separating wall was displaced south to divide the external window into separate sections, lighting both the study and the stairs. This modification resulted in the door to the saloon being displaced south, to align correctly with the new position of the internal window. To ensure symmetry in the saloon, the southern displacement of the door to the study required a corresponding displacement of the door to the china closet. As the door to the china closet was moved south its window also had to have its internal frame moved south, to remain in line with the door. This resulted in the central axis of the room also being moved south as its half-way line was determined by the centre of the door and window. This gave a little extra space at the north end of the room which Chambers filled with an alcove framed by the arch. This complex interaction between separate spaces indicates the remarkable complexity of co-ordinating the interiors of the Casino.

right: *The zodiac room*

THE STATE ROOM

On the first floor one discovers the remarkable conceit of inserting the most ornate interior in the Casino in a position that can be reached only by the essentially practical stairs. On climbing the stairs the first suggestion of a different character is found in the fine rococo shell in plaster on the staircase ceiling. Naturalistic and disproportionately large, it has little if anything to relate it to the Roman inspiration of the interior decoration on the ground floor, and Chambers's antique monumentality is a world away. Furthermore, at the head of the stairs, the first floor corridor, multi-levelled and unpretentious, betrays nothing of the riches to be found.

The state room, the most colourful interior of the Casino, betrays a mood distinct from any other formal interior in the Casino. Decorated in green and white with gilding to the details, and with a screen of columns, the state room is at once more extravagant and more architectural. The appreciation of restraint and understatement, so important to the rooms on the ground floor, is here replaced by an extravagant display of wealth. Yet despite its ostentation the room is one of the most comfortable interiors in the Casino. The scale is homely, neither cramped nor overlarge, the space is interesting, without being playful or artificial, and the detail is quite relaxed, avoiding the intense discipline typical of Chambers. Indeed the lack of sophistication suggests the hand of Vierpyl rather than that most tasteful of architects. The room's probable inspiration is Lady Suffolk's bedchamber at Marble Hill, Middlesex. They have similar designs of a columnar screen separating a reception space from the bed, with flat and coved ceilings further distinguishing the two spaces. This would suggest Chambers's involvement at an early stage.

Determining the precise character of the original room has been particularly difficult here as this whole floor suffered significant damage before the Casino was taken into state care. The gilding has not been proved conclusively to be original. The colouring is not securely dated to the 1770s. It is known to have been fashionable at that time but the fragments on which it is based may date from the nineteenth century. The original heaviness of the interior has survived, with simple uncarved mouldings to the skirting and the chair-rail.

INFORMAL ROOMS

There is an elegant simplicity to the other first-floor rooms, where the potentially awkward spaces are uncommonly successful. These rooms have simple but refined details, including cupboards set into window surrounds to enhance the proportions of the frames. Leading from the corridor is the small staircase to the roof, distinguished by Chinese style fretwork supporting the handrail.

In the basement plain vaulted spaces contain the kitchen and ancillary service areas. These have the clear and clean elegance characteristic of such rooms. Rounded mouldings enrich the lines of the vaulting and the plain stone corbels carrying the vaults have a functional directness, as much a part of eighteenth century design as any of Chambers's ceilings.

Indeed the practicalities of design are of particular importance in the Casino even if appearances are the priority. Chambers sets the down-pipes from the gutters inside the corner columns so as not to spoil any of the four fronts of the building. The columns reappear in the basement where, as pipes for internal drainage, they can be checked for blockage by the removal of curved wooden doors in their sides. Outside the building, the urns are drilled with inconspicuous holes to allow water to escape from any hollows in their design, and the lowest step at each flight is channelled to catch and drain water, helping to keep the ground around the Casino dry.

CONCLUSION

Though Charlemont's extensive estates and collections have been dispersed in the years since his death, the Casino remains as a testament to his enlightened philosophy. Its adoption as a national monument by the Office of Public Works in the 1930s and its restoration in the 1970s are a clear reminder of his continued significance today through his most tangible contribution to Ireland.

FOR FURTHER READING

John Cornforth, 'The Casino at Marino, Dublin', *Country Life*, Feb. 4 and Feb. 11, 1988

Maurice Craig, *The Volunteer Earl*, London, 1948

John Harris, *Sir William Chambers, Knight of the Polar Star*, London, 1970

David Newman Johnson, 'The Casino at Marino', *Irish Arts Review*, Autumn 1984

John Redmill and Ian C Bristow, 'The Casino at Marino, Dublin', *Transactions of the Association for Studies in the Conservation of Historic Buildings*, Vol. 9